PHYSICAL SCIENCE IN DEPTH

ELECTRICITY AND ELECTRICAL CIRCUITS

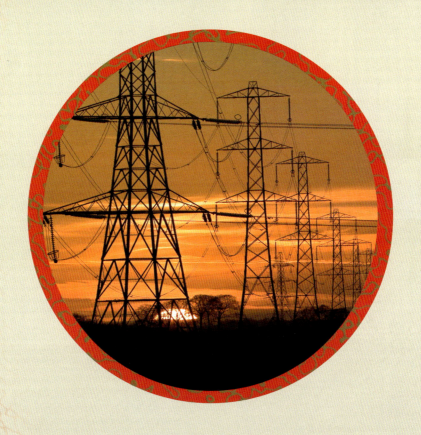

Sally Morgan

www.heinemann.co.uk/library
Visit our website to find out more infor...

To order:
☎ Phone 44 (0) 1865 888066
🖹 Send a fax to 44 (0) 1865 314091
🖳 Visit the Heinemann bookshop at www...
   our catalogue and order online.

First published in Great Britain by
Heinemann Library, Halley Court, Jordan Hill,
Oxford OX2 8EJ, part of Harcourt Education.
Heinemann is a registered trademark of
Harcourt Education Ltd.

Produced for Heinemann Library by
White-Thomson Publishing Ltd
Editorial: Sarah Shannon, Patrick Catel,
and Catherine Clarke
Design: Richard Parker and Tinstar Design Ltd
   www.tinstar.co.uk
Illustrations: Kerry Flaherty and Q2A Solutions
Picture Research: Amy Sparks
Production: Duncan Gilbert

Originated by Modern Age Repro
Printed and bound in China by South China
   Printing Company

ISBN: 978 0 4310 8107 6
12 11 10 09 08
10 9 8 7 6 5 4 3 2 1

British Library Cataloguing in Publication Data
Morgan, Sally
Electricity and electrical circuits. - (Physical science
in depth)
537
A full catalogue record for this book is available
from the British Library.

Acknowledgements
The publishers would like to thank the following
for permission to reproduce photographs:
Corbis pp. **12** (Charles E. Rotkin), **13** (Paul A.
Souders), **21** (Steve Allen/Brand X Pictures),
30 (Everett Kennedy/Brown/epa), **31** (Owen
Franken), **33** (Jason Reed/Reuters), **34** (Richard T.
Nowitz), **36** (Rick Friedman), **37** (Pixland),
43 (Alison Wright), **53** (Car Culture), **55** (John
Gress/Reuters), **56** (Mario Ruiz/ZUMA), **57** (Roger
Ressmeyer), **59** (Everett Kennedy/Brown/epa);
Ecoscene pp. **23** (David Wootton Photography),
46 (Judyth Platt); Getty Images pp. **5** (Mitchell
Funk/Photographer's Choice), **11** (Hulton Archive),
49 (Peter Kramer); iStockphoto.com pp. **7**
(blaneyphoto/Nathan Blaney); **10** (Moritz von
Hacht), **16** (Ben Conlan), **17** (M. Eric Honeycutt),
19 (Thomas Mounsey), **26** (Matthew Cole),
41 (Harris Shiffman), **47** (Vegard Berget), **48** (Skip
O'Donnell), **50** (Andrew Johnson), **52** (Tom Young);
Photolibrary (Mark Deeble and Victoria Stone/OSF)
p. **39**; Science Photo Library pp. **9** (Charles D.
Winters), **14** (Andrew Lambert Photography),
25 (Peter Menzel), **38** (Gary Meszaros); Topfoto
(Imageworks) p. **27**.

Cover photograph of the skyline of Sydney,
Australia, lit up at night reproduced with permission
of BrandXPictures.

The publishers would like to thank Ann and Patrick
Fullick and Mike Goldsmith for their assistance in
the preparation of this book.

Every effort has been made to contact copyright
holders of any material reproduced in this book. Any
omissions will be rectified in subsequent printings if
notice is given to the publishers.

Disclaimer

All the Internet addresses (URLs) given in this book
were valid at the time of going to press. However, due to
the dynamic nature of the Internet, some addresses may
have changed, or sites may have ceased to exist since
publication. While the author and publishers regret any
inconvenience this may cause readers, no responsibility
for any such changes can be accepted by either the author
or the publishers.

MORGAN, Sally

Electricity and
electrical circuits

Contents

Words printed in the text in bold, like this,
are explained in the glossary.

A world of electricity

Look around you. How many things can you see that are powered by electricity? Modern life is completely dependent on electricity. We simply cannot do without our lights, televisions, computers, fridges, and freezers. In fact, when the electricity goes off in a modern city there is chaos!

Electricity is a form of **energy**. Electrical energy is particularly useful because it can be easily changed into other forms of energy, such as light, sound, and movement. Electricity is not just man-made but also occurs naturally. Lightning, for example, is a form of electrical energy. Human bodies rely on electrical signals that move along **nerves** carrying messages to and from the brain. Some animals even use electricity as a weapon.

A wide variety of energy sources can be used to generate electricity. Much of the world's electricity is generated using **fossil fuels** such as oil, gas, and coal. About one-fifth of electricity is generated in **nuclear power** stations, which are powered by uranium. Other energy sources include wind, waves, rushing water, and the Sun. These are called **renewable** energy sources because they will never run out. In contrast, fossil fuels are non-renewable and they cannot be replaced. As fossil fuels become more scarce, more electricity will have to come from renewable resources.

Did you know..?

More than 1.6 billion people in the world do not have access to electricity. That is one quarter of the world's population. If you could look at the world at night from an aeroplane, you would see that much of Europe and North America is lit up, but most of Africa and Asia would be completely covered in darkness.

This book explains the nature of electricity: what it is, and how it behaves. It looks at different types of electrical **circuits** and how electricity can be generated. It also investigates the role of electrical signals in the human body and the way electricity and medicine are linked. This book will also touch upon the future of electricity, and introduce you to some of the exciting projects concerned with electricity that are being carried out around the world.

The millions of lights on the strip in Las Vegas, USA, are lit 24 hours a day. This uses up a lot of electricity, much of which comes from a local coal-fired power station.

What is electricity?

Electricity is a form of energy, just like sound and light. A bolt of lightning that flashes across the sky is a type of electricity, as is the shock you get when you touch a light switch after walking across a carpeted floor. To understand electricity and how it works, it is important to know where it comes from.

All **matter** is made up of tiny particles called **atoms**. An atom is incredibly small – far too small to be seen with the naked eye. In fact, it is only just possible to see an atom using the very latest powerful microscopes. Scientists have discovered that atoms are made up of even smaller particles called **protons**, **neutrons**, and **electrons**.

To understand how these particles are arranged in an atom, imagine you are looking at our solar system. The Sun is at the centre, and all the planets are in **orbit** around it. The Sun is the equivalent of the **nucleus** in an atom, while the planets are the equivalent of the electrons. This is the centre of the atom, which is made up of protons and neutrons. These two particles are quite heavy. That is why most of the **mass** of the atom is in the nucleus. Orbiting the nucleus are a number of tiny electrons. Each electron has such a small mass that it can hardly be measured.

Protons and neutrons are found in the nucleus at the centre of an atom. The electrons form a cloud around the nucleus.

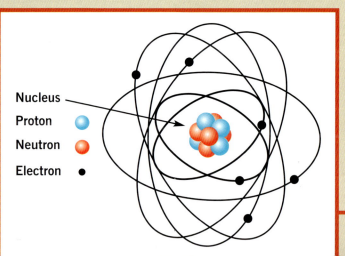

Nucleus
Proton
Neutron
Electron

KEY EXPERIMENT Observing electricity

The first observations of electricity date back to the time of ancient Greece. A Greek philosopher, Thales of Miletus (640–546 BC), noticed that the pretty orange stone called amber behaved oddly. When he rubbed a piece of amber with a woollen cloth, small objects such as dust, feathers, and bits of straw stuck to the stone. He did not know it, but he was observing **static electricity**.

This orange stone is amber. Thousands of years ago, amber played an important role in the understanding of static electricity.

Both protons and electrons carry a charge that may attract or **repel** another particle. Protons have a positive charge, and electrons have a negative charge. Neutrons have no charge. In an atom, the number of protons equals the number of electrons. All the positive charges are balanced out by all the negative charges so the atom has no overall charge. Atoms can easily lose or gain an electron. When an atom loses an electron it is left with one more proton than it has electrons, so it has an overall positive charge. If an atom gains an electron, it has an overall negative charge.

Did you know..?

The word electricity comes from the Greek word *elector*, which means "beaming sun". The word electron means "amber": the stone that interested Thales of Miletus.

STATIC ELECTRICITY

You have probably observed static electricity many times. It may cause your clothes to stick together when you pull them out of the tumble dryer or make your hair stick to a woolly hat as you pull it off.

You can investigate static electricity further by carrying out simple experiments in which different materials are rubbed together. For example, if a glass rod is rubbed with a piece of silk, the silk and the glass are attracted to each other. But if two glass rods are rubbed with silk and then placed close together, the glass rods push away from (repel) each other. The strange behaviour of the glass rod and the piece of silk is caused by the movement of electrons.

When the glass rod is rubbed with silk, electrons are transferred between the two materials. One is left with a positive charge, and the other left with a negative charge, so they are attracted to each other. However, when two glass rods are rubbed with silk, both rods are left with the same charge so they repel each other. When you pull off a woolly hat, the hat rubs against your hair, gains electrons, and becomes negatively charged. The hair is left with a positive charge. Positive and negative attract, which is why the hat attracts your hair.

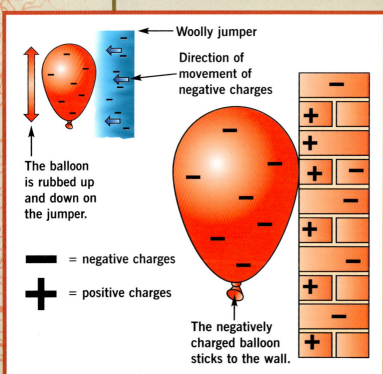

Woolly jumper

Direction of movement of negative charges

The balloon is rubbed up and down on the jumper.

━━ = negative charges

✚ = positive charges

The negatively charged balloon sticks to the wall.

If you rub a balloon on a woolly jumper, electrons move from the jumper to the balloon. The balloon can then stick to a wall. This is because its extra, negatively charged electrons are attracted to positive charges in the atoms of the wall.

The protons and neutrons in an atom are held tightly together in the nucleus. The electrons, however, are spinning around outside of the nucleus – sometimes very far away. For example, if you imagined an atom to be the size of a football stadium, the nucleus would be the size of a pea at the centre of the stadium. The rest of the space would be occupied by the electrons. Because of this distance, it is relatively easy to attract the furthest electrons from one atom to another.

KEY EXPERIMENT Make a magic wand

You can find out more about static electricity by making a "magic wand". On a dry day, take a plastic pen or a length of plastic rod and rub it hard with a woolly sock or other piece of wool. Place a table-tennis ball on a table and move the wand close to it. Watch how the ball moves away. Rub the wand again and place it near a running tap. Turn the tap until there is only a narrow stream of water flowing. Watch how the water moves towards your wand. All of these "magic" effects are due to static electricity caused by the wool rubbing the plastic.

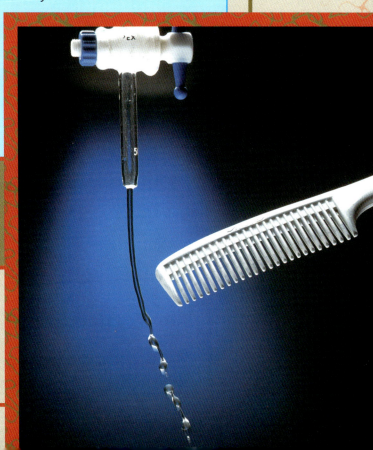

This plastic comb has been rubbed with wool and become charged. When the comb is held close to the tap it attracts the stream of water, which has an opposite charge.

LIGHTNING

Lightning is one of the most impressive examples of static electricity. It is also one of the most deadly. Lightning is caused by a massive build-up of electrical charges in a storm cloud. When the charges jump from the cloud to the ground, or to other clouds, there is a huge **electrical discharge** and a bolt of lightning is seen in the sky.

During a storm, particles of water and ice in a cloud are moved around by air currents. As the particles collide with one another, electrons are knocked away from their atoms. The resulting positively and negatively charged particles collect in different areas of the cloud. When a negatively charged area of the cloud moves close to Earth, it causes the ground to become electrically charged. Negative charges move away from the cloud, leaving positive charges closest to the cloud. Electrons jump from the cloud to the ground, causing a bolt of lightning.

Electrons may also jump from cloud to cloud, causing the type of lightning bolts that zigzag across the sky. The energy from lightning causes the surrounding air to expand very quickly and this produces a thunderclap.

Every second, 100 bolts of lightning strike around the world. Each bolt produces a bright flash of light and temperatures of up to 30,000°C (54,032°F). A single bolt contains enough electrical energy to power a small town for a year.

SCIENCE PIONEERS Benjamin Franklin: Lightning

In 1752, American inventor Benjamin Franklin (1706–1790) attached a metal key to a silk kite and flew the kite high in the sky during a storm. When a thundercloud moved close to the kite, an electric spark jumped across to the key. When he put his hand near the key, Franklin felt an electric shock and saw sparks: thus proving that lightning was really electricity. Though his experiment proved that lightning was caused by electricity, Franklin took a tremendous risk in trying such a stunt. He could easily have been killed. Other scientists who tried to repeat this experiment did die.

STRUCK BY LIGHTNING

When lightning strikes Earth, it is most likely to hit the tallest objects. For this reason, tall buildings are fitted with lightning rods. These metal rods are placed at the highest part of a structure. They stick up from the top of the building and run all the way down into the ground. Then if lightning were to strike the building, it would hit the rod first and be safely **conducted** to the ground.

Although the chances of a person being struck by lightning are very slim, hundreds of people are killed or seriously injured by lightning each year.

Before someone is struck by lightning, they usually feel a tingling sensation on their skin as their hairs stand on end. After being struck, the victim usually suffers extensive burns and nerve damage. They may also suffer memory loss and even a change in personality.

USING STATIC ELECTRICITY

Static electricity can build up all around us. Simply sitting on a chair can produce static. Although static electricity can be very annoying and give us small shocks, it has lots of uses in everyday life.

CLEANING AIR

A filter called an electrostatic precipitator uses static electricity to reduce air pollution caused by factory chimneys. Here's how it works:

• Dirty air contains tiny dirt particles as well as gases and water. When the tiny particles of dirt bump into the gases and water, they lose electrons and are left with a positive charge.

• The filter has a negative charge, so it attracts the dust particles as they pass through the chimney. The dust is collected before it can escape into the atmosphere.

This power plant in Memphis, Tennessee, USA, uses electrostatic precipitators (filters) in its chimneys to help prevent pollution.

A device called an air ionizer uses a similar principle to freshen the air inside buildings. As air is drawn into the ionizer, the device removes electrons from the dust and other particles in the air. The positively charged particles then stick to the inside of the ionizer, which has a negative charge.

PHOTOCOPIERS

Photocopiers use static electricity to make copies of documents. Inside the photocopier is a drum that can be charged with static electricity, just like a balloon when it is rubbed on a woolly jumper. The photocopy is made using fine black powder called toner. The document to be copied is scanned by a laser, which charges up the drum in a mirror image of the ink on the paper. When the drum is charged, it attracts the toner, which is rolled on to a piece of paper and heated to fix it in place.

CASE STUDY Van de Graaff generator

The Van de Graaff **generator** is a strange machine that can generate very large amounts of static electricity. It was invented by the American scientist Robert Van de Graaff (1901–1967) in 1920. The generator is made up of a **motor** that drives a belt around two rollers. The rollers are attached to a metal dome over one end. As the belt rubs on the rollers it causes a lot of negative charges to collect on the dome. When a person places their hand on the dome, the negative charges flow through the person's body causing their hair to stand on end.

The static from the Van de Graaff generator is making this girl's hair stand on end. Each individual hair receives a negative charge, so they repel each other.

PREVENTING STATIC

Static can build up whenever two different materials rub against each other. A conveyor belt in a factory can build up static, so can clothes in a tumble dryer. In many industrial processes static is unwanted.

Controlling the build up of static electricity in some industries, such as an electronics factory or in computer-chip manufacturing, is very important. An electric charge can harm employees, damage equipment, or attract dust and contaminate products. Employees wear anti-static wristbands or heel straps, or even rub their skin with anti-static hand cream. These types of factory may also have anti-static mats on the floors.

AVOIDING STATIC

Static shocks are worst when the air is dry. Static doesn't build up on damp days because there is a lot of moisture in the air, so one way to reduce static in the home or office is to use a humidifier.

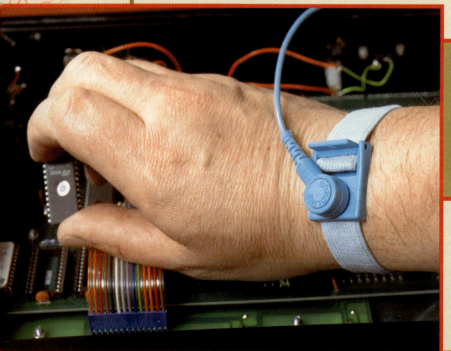

The blue plastic band on this computer technician's wrist prevents the build up of static as he works on this computer. This is important as a static discharge could damage the computer and lose data.

You can also avoid static shocks by wearing wool or cotton clothing. Clothes made from **synthetic** fibres, such as polyester and nylon, are more likely to cause static build-up than those made from natural fibres. People often get a shock as they get out of a car because they have built up static by sitting on the car seat. The best way to avoid a shock in this case is to touch the glass window before getting out of the car, or to hold the metal part of the door, so that the charges can escape to Earth.

DANGER AT THE PETROL PUMP

Another risky situation occurs when petrol is pumped from tankers into underground tanks at filling stations. The flow of fuel along the pipes causes **friction**: the **force** that results when two objects are rubbed together. This can cause a build up of static electricity. This is dangerous because the fuel is highly flammable, and it can easily be ignited by a single spark and cause an explosion.

To reduce the risk, a special **grounding** device is fitted to the pipe in order to allow the electrical charges to flow harmlessly to Earth before they can build up. Mobile phones can produce static electricity. Although there is a very small risk from mobile phones, most petrol stations have a warning sign telling people not to use their mobile phone while filling up with petrol.

Did you know..?

The most common way for a fire to start when someone is filling their car with petrol occurs when the person gets in or out of the car while the petrol is still being pumped into the tank. Static builds up on the person's body when they rub against the car seat. When the person touches the metal nozzle of the pump handle, an electric discharge is produced. When that spark jumps to the nozzle it can ignite the petrol. A good way to avoid this is to touch the metal of the car door before touching the pump nozzle.

Moving electricity

Static electricity is not the only form of electricity. Another form is called **current electricity**. This is the form of electricity that is supplied to homes to power lights and electrical equipment. This form of electricity is different from static electricity. In static electricity the charges (electrons) build up in one place. Though the charges may jump between objects, they do not create a **current** (flow of electrons from one place to another). Once scientists discovered they could pass current electricity along wires, it opened up the possibility of using electricity in many different and useful ways.

CURRENTS AND VOLTAGE

A current of electricity flows easily through a **conductor** such as metal in a wire. Current electricity needs to flow along a loop, or circuit, so that the charges can be returned to their original position and be recycled. There cannot be any gaps in the circuit because the electrons creating the current cannot jump across large gaps. Current electricity also requires something to push the electrons along the conductor, since they will not start moving of their own accord. This pushing power, known as **voltage**, is provided by a **battery** or a generator.

AA batteries are often used in small electronic devices, such as portable CD players and remote controls.

Voltage is a measure of how much energy is given to electrons to make them move. An energy source such as a battery gives the electrons a certain amount of "push". The larger the voltage, the bigger the push. The voltage tells you how much power a current can deliver, so the bigger the voltage the more power can be delivered. If you look on the side of a battery, you will see a number indicating the voltage (V) of the battery. Many small batteries, such as A, AA, and AAA sizes, provide 1.5V.

AMPERES

A current is created by a flow of electrons, with each electron carrying a tiny negative charge. There needs to be many millions of electrons flowing through a wire to create a sufficient charge to power a torch for example, and even more is needed to power a washing machine. The size of a current is measured in units called **amperes** (A). An **ammeter** is a device that can measure the current.

Another unit that may be seen on a battery is ampere-hour. This value tells you how long the battery should last. A typical 1.5V AA battery may have a value of 1 ampere-hour. (It may be shown as 1,000 milli-ampere-hours.) This would tell you that if your circuit drew a current of 0.1 amps, the battery would last 10 hours.

WATTS

Voltage tells you how much energy is provided by a battery; a **watt** is a unit that measures power. A 1.5V battery could probably deliver about 1.5 watts of power. Large household appliances, such as electric ovens and electric fires, need several thousand watts to operate, so mains electricity supplies are produced at much higher voltages: 220–240V in Europe and 110V in the United States.

It takes a lot of energy to provide all the electricity needed to light a home – and run electrical appliances.

MAKING CIRCUITS

A circuit is a loop around which an electric current can flow. An example of a very simple circuit is a battery linked by wires to a small torch lamp. When the circuit is complete, the current flows from the battery along the wire and lights up the lamp. Often circuits have a switch, which is a simple device that either completes the circuit or breaks it to stop the current.

WIRED IN SERIES

The components in a circuit can be wired up in different ways. Imagine you want to make a circuit with three light bulbs. You could connect them up one after the other in a row, using lengths of wire to connect them. This makes a series circuit. In this type of circuit, if one light bulb fails all the other lights also go off. The failure of one bulb means the circuit is broken and the current cannot flow.

WIRED IN PARALLEL

Another way to wire up the three light bulbs is in parallel. Each light bulb is in a different loop, forcing the current to flow down three different paths. This time if one of the light bulbs fail, the other two stay on. This type of circuit is used in homes, so that if an appliance or light on one loop fails, the other loops continue to operate normally.

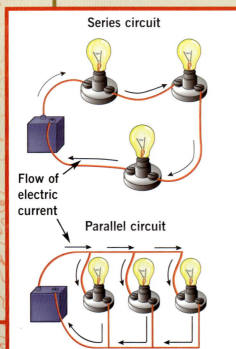

Series circuit

Flow of electric current

Parallel circuit

In a series circuit, all of the bulbs are connected, one after the other, on one circuit. A parallel circuit is more practical because each bulb lies on its own circuit and doesn't rely on the other bulbs to work.

INTEGRATED CIRCUITS

An integrated circuit is a very advanced type of circuit. Integrated circuits are used in many hi-tech appliances, such as alarm systems, computers, MP3 players, and mobile phones. The term "integrated" comes from the fact that all the components are constructed together on the same chip. The chip is made from silicon, a type of **semiconductor**. The details of the circuits are microscopically small, so the distances between the components are tiny and the electric current can flow quickly between them.

KEY EXPERIMENT Making a lemon battery

A lemon contains an acidic liquid that is perfect for conducting electricity, so the fruit can be used as a battery. To make a lemon battery, push two **electrodes** into the lemon. One electrode can be made of a galvanized (iron covered by zinc) nail and the other a thick piece of copper wire. Connect the electrodes to an ammeter to see how much electricity is generated. You can also add a small light bulb to the circuit, which should light up. Try using two lemons to increase the amount of electricity produced by your battery. Link the two lemons with another set of electrodes.

The reading on the ammeter shows that the lemon is generating enough voltage to produce a small current.

CONDUCTORS AND INSULATORS

Conductors are very important in electricity. They are materials that allow an electric current to flow easily. Without a conductor, there cannot be an electric current. **Insulators** do just the opposite – they are materials that do not allow electricity to flow through them. Glass, rubber, and plastic are all good insulators.

Although they are good at preventing the flow of electricity, insulators can allow a build up of static. That is because the electrons are held in by the material. Conductors, however, allow electricity to flow through them, so they do not build up static charges.

Metals, such as silver, aluminum, and mercury, make some of the best conductors. Copper, another type of metal, is a particularly good conductor and is used to make wires. It is dangerous to touch a bare wire carrying a current, so the wire is encased in plastic. The plastic is an insulator. It stops the electricity escaping from the wire and makes the wire safe for us to touch. Wind and air are also insulators.

RESISTANCE

All conductors resist the flow of electrons to some extent. That is, they slow down the movement of the electrons, making it more difficult for the current to pass. The level of **resistance** is measured in units called Ohms. As resistance increases, it becomes harder for the electrons to move through the conductor. Whenever there is resistance, some energy is wasted because some of the electrical energy is converted to heat. This also causes the conductor to become hot.

Resistance can be used to control the size of a current. Using a component called a **resistor** can be useful in some circuits. For example, resistors are used in radios. When you turn the volume dial you are actually changing the resistance, which in turn increases or decreases the volume. A resistor is made from coils of a high-resistance metal. Each resistor is designed so that it can produce a known level of resistance to ensure that the correct amount of current flows around a circuit.

SUPERCONDUCTORS

As the temperature of a conductor decreases, its resistance also falls. Some materials, when cooled below a certain critical temperature, have no resistance at all. The electrons can move through the conductor without wasting any energy. This means that there is more electrical energy available for use. As the temperature of a conductor decreases, its resistance also falls. Some materials, when cooled below a particular critical temperature, have no resistance at all. This temperature is usually about -253°C (-423°F). Recently, some materials have been discovered that superconduct at temperatures of -143°C (-225°F) – the highest known critical temperature. However, none have been discovered that will superconduct at room temperature.

Superconductors have a number of uses. However, because the superconductors have to be cooled to such low temperatures, their uses are very specialized. For example, superconductors are used on Maglev trains where the train floats above a superconducting magnet (see page 30) and in medical equipment such as magnetic resonance imaging (MRI) scanners (see page 31).

The latest superconductors are used in power station generators where they help to generate electricity as efficiently as possible.

SAFE CIRCUITS

Electricity is essential to modern life, but it can be dangerous. Faulty wiring is one of the leading causes of fire in the home. A circuit can be overloaded if it draws too much current, for example if too many appliances are plugged into the same circuit. This can cause heat to build up, which may start a fire. To prevent this from happening, circuits contain safety devices that stop the current if a fault develops. The most common of these safety devices is the **fuse**.

FUSES

A simple fuse consists of a piece of wire in a protective case, and can be found in plugs, electrical devices, and fuse boxes. The wire inside the fuse has a low melting point, so if the current becomes too great for the circuit, the wire gets hot and melts. This breaks the circuit and the current stops. The circuit can only be re-established when the melted fuse is replaced.

CIRCUIT BREAKERS

A **circuit breaker** is a type of fuse that is found close to where the mains electricity comes into a building. Its role is to break the circuit if the current gets too large. A circuit breaker is an improvement on a simple fuse because it is more sensitive and faster to react, and can detect very small faults. It can also be reset by flipping a switch and therefore doesn't have to be replaced every time it is tripped. Circuit breakers are fitted in most homes.

CASE STUDY Light bulbs

It is important to use the right type of light bulb in a lamp fitting. Most lamps and other light fittings have labels stating the maximum wattage of bulb that should be fitted. If the bulb used is too powerful, the heat from the bulb could melt the fitting and cause a fire. The power of a bulb is measured in watts as this is roughly equivalent to the amount of light they produce. A dim bulb may use 40W and a bright one 100W.

MULTIMETERS

A multimeter is a useful device that can measure and find faults in electrical circuits. It measures voltage (volts), and resistance (ohms), and some can measure current (amps). The meter is attached to a circuit by two leads or crocodile clips. The main dial selects the type of measurement required. To measure the voltage between two points in a circuit, the clips need to touch the points. To measure the resistance between two points the circuit must be disconnected and the battery of the multimeter used to provide the voltage needed to calculate the resistance. Current is usually measured by a special meter that can measure the electromagnetic field created by the current as it flows through the wire (see page 27). When fault finding, it is important to know the expected readings. If the readings differ from the expected, then there is a fault on the circuit.

This person is using a multimeter to check the electrical circuits in a circuit box. The box contains the circuit breakers and wires that link to the circuits in an entire building.

DIRECT CURRENTS

In a circuit powered by a battery, the current of electrons flows continually in one direction from the negative terminal of the battery, through the circuit, and back to the positive terminal. This is called a **direct current** (DC). There is another type of current electricity, however, called an **alternating current** (AC).

ALTERNATING CURRENT

An alternating current is one in which the direction of the current changes as many as 120 times per second. One moment the electrons are moving in one direction, and the next they are moving in the opposite direction. It is the continual changing of the current's direction that creates the alternating current.

Electrons always flow from a negative terminal to a positive one. This means an alternating current can be created by continually switching over the terminals. A terminal may be positive one moment and negative the next. The negatively charged electrons are attracted towards the positive terminal and when the positive terminal becomes negative, the electrons are repelled and they move away.

THE BATTLE OF THE CURRENTS

Electricity was first being generated on a large scale towards the end of the 19th century. At that time, it was all direct current. However, scientists discovered that there was a problem transmitting the electricity over long distances. The resistance in the wires was causing a loss of power. In 1887 American George Westinghouse (1846–1914), working with Nikola Tesla (see box), developed a way of transmitting electricity over long distances using a high-voltage alternating current (AC). From that time onwards an alternating current was used to transmit electricity.

Today DC has new advantages. The use of semiconductors and integrated circuits in computers, televisions, and microwaves means that these pieces of equipment need to have an internal DC power supply and a device called an inverter that converts the incoming AC to DC. In addition, some of the systems used to generate electricity from renewable energy sources, such as solar panels fitted with **photovoltaic cells**, can only generate DC electricity.

SCIENCE PIONEERS
Nikola Tesla: Alternating Currents

Inventor and scientist Nikola Tesla (1856–1943) was born in Serbia but later moved to the United States. He invented many devices, including spark plugs for engines, pumps, **turbines**, and **compressors**. He even carried out some of the earliest research into robotics. One of Tesla's most important inventions was a motor that produced an alternating current. In 1888 he worked for George Westinghouse and together they devised the system for distributing electricity using AC.

The Tesla coil, invented by Nikola Tesla, can produce a very high voltage spark of electricity, rather like lightning. Large Tesla coils use mains electricity at 240V to produce a spark of one million volts.

Electricity and magnetism

There are many similarities between **magnetism** and electricity. We learned that electricity is about positive and negative charges that attract or repel each other. Similarly, magnetism is based on attraction and repulsion between the poles of a magnet. Magnets have a **magnetic field**. Similarly, there is a force field around any electrically charged material that affects other charged objects. This is called the electric field.

MAGNETS

A magnet has a north pole and a south pole. If you've ever played with magnets, you know that when you bring the north pole of one magnet close to the south pole of another, the two magnets become attracted to each other and stick together. But if you try to put a north pole of a magnet close to another north pole you can feel a force pushing them away from each other. The two magnets are repelling each other. Poles that are the same (north and north, or south and south) repel each other and different poles (north and south) attract each other.

Magnets have an invisible field of force around them, which is known as the magnetic field. This is the area in which the magnet can cause a push or pull, and it runs from the north to the south pole. There is also a gigantic magnetic field around Earth. It is the attraction of Earth's magnetic field that causes a compass to line up pointing north to south.

The iron filings in this photo show the magnetic field around the bar magnet.

SCIENCE PIONEERS Hans Oersted: Electromagnetism

In 1820, Danish scientist Hans Oersted (1777–1851) was the first to describe electromagnetism. Quite by chance, he noticed that when an electric current flowed along a wire it caused a nearby compass needle to move away from north. This intrigued him and he carried out a number of experiments. Soon, he was able to prove that a magnetic field is created when a wire carries an electric current.

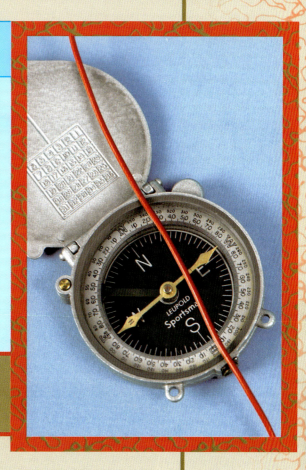

The electric current running through this wire is causing the compass to point in the direction of the wire's magnetic field.

ELECTROMAGNETS

An **electromagnet** is a magnet created by electricity. When an electric current is passed along a coil of wire, called a **solenoid**, it generates a magnetic field. The force of the magnetic field can be made larger by having more coils. An even stronger electromagnet is made by placing a rod of iron through the middle of the coil. This turns the iron into a magnet, so the force of the magnetic field is increased. Electromagnets are useful because they can be switched on and off instantly. They have many everyday uses in switches and bells. They are also found in disk drives of computers and electric motors in hairdryers, vacuum cleaners, washing machines and electric lawnmowers, and much more.

USING ELECTROMAGNETS

Today, electromagnets have many important uses in industry. They are found in scrapyards where they separate out and lift iron and steel from other metals. They are found in power stations where they generate electricity (see page 40), in motors, and in maglev trains. These are trains that make use of **magnetic levitation** as they are lifted just above the tracks by an electromagnet (see page 30).

THE ELECTRIC BELL

A doorbell is a very simple example of an everyday use of an electromagnet. An electric doorbell contains a bell, a hammer or striker on a spring, a bell push, and an electromagnet. The bell push is the switch. When someone presses the bell push, the circuit is completed and a current flows through the electromagnet. This creates a magnetic field. The magnetism attracts a piece of iron that is attached to the hammer. The end of the hammer is pulled across and strikes the bell. As soon as this happens, the circuit is broken and the electromagnet loses its magnetism. The piece of iron is dropped back to its original position, and the spring moves the hammer back into place.

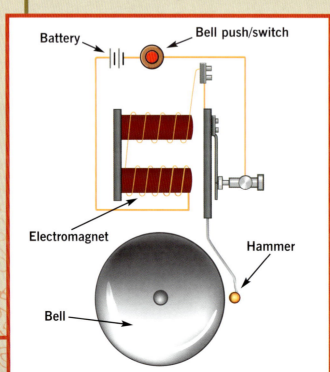

Battery

Bell push/switch

Electromagnet

Hammer

Bell

When the button on a doorbell is pushed, a current flows through the wire, creating a magnetic force that attracts the iron bar. The iron bar then causes the hammer to strike the bell.

THE ELECTRIC MOTOR

A motor is a machine that changes electrical energy into mechanical energy (motion). This motion is used to move the parts of a machine, such as an electric lawnmower, a car, or a train.

Electromagnetism is the basis of all motors. Inside a simple motor are two permanent magnets and an electromagnet made from a loop of wire. The electric current flows in on one side of the loop and out through the other. When the electric current is switched on, the magnetic field of the electromagnet interacts with the magnetic field of the permanent magnets. On one side of the loop, the interaction pushes the loop up, while on the other side the loop is pushed down, so the loop spins. To keep the loop spinning in the same direction an alternating current is needed. It is the spinning that turns the motor.

A direct current from a battery can also be used to provide the electricity for a motor. However, in that case, the motor would need to contain a device called a commutator to keep reversing the current at just the right moment.

In an electric motor, the direction of the current changes each time the loop of wire turns halfway, reversing the direction of the loop's magnetic field. This means that, wherever the loop is, its north pole is always closest to the north pole of the permanent magnet, so it is always pushed away, and keeps spinning.

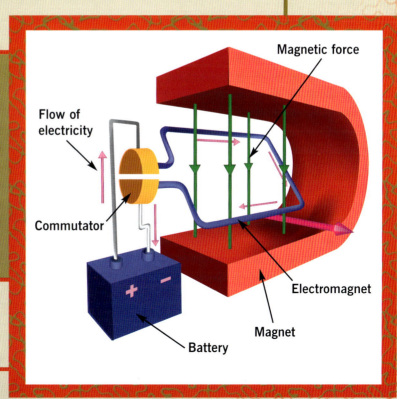

Magnetic force

Flow of electricity

Commutator

Electromagnet

Magnet

Battery

MAGLEV TRAINS

A maglev train speeds along a track without ever touching the rails. The train floats a few centimetres above the track and is held in place by electromagnetism. Here's how it works: Imagine you have two magnets. You place one on a table and hold the other in your hand. As you bring the north pole of the magnet in your hand close to the north pole of the magnet on the table, the repulsion between the two north poles causes the magnet in your hand to be pushed away. This is how the train is lifted off the track – there is an electromagnet in the train and another in the track. When both electromagnets are switched on, the train is lifted above the track and pushed forwards by an electric motor. The train does not touch the track, so there is no friction between the two. This enables the train to travel at very high speeds.

Maglev trains date back to the 1950s when a British scientist, Eric Laithwaite, demonstrated magnetic levitation. Today the maglev trains in Japan and Germany travel at speeds in excess of 550 kilometres (342 miles) per hour. Although constructing and running maglev systems is very expensive, the trains are a low noise and pollution-free method of transport.

In 2003 this maglev train in Japan set a world record when it reached a maximum speed of 581 kilometres (361 miles) per hour on an experimental track.

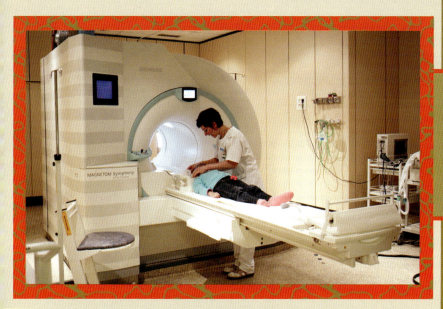

A patient lies on a table ready to go into the MRI scanner. How far in the patient must go depends on the area of the body being scanned.

MAGNETIC RESONANCE IMAGING

A magnetic resonance imaging (MRI) scanner is a tool that doctors use to get a very detailed picture of the inside of a body. Unlike an X-ray, which only shows a person's bones, an MRI image shows a patient's soft tissues and organs. It can also show blood flowing through a person's body.

The basic setup for an MRI machine is a huge magnetic cube that has a horizontal tube running through it. A patient lies down on a table that slides into the tube. As the patient is being scanned, the machine creates a point-by-point image using magnetic fields and radio waves. Then the points are put together to create either a two-dimensional image or a three-dimensional model of the patient's body. Doctors use these images to detect disease and surgeons use them to get an idea of what they can expect to find during an operation.

Did you know..?

Electromagnets can be used in hospitals to remove tiny fragments of iron and steel stuck in people's eyes after an accident.

Animal electricity

Lightning is not the only example of electricity in nature. Animals use electricity in many ways. Many animals, including humans, have a nervous system. This is an internal communications network made up of the brain and nerves. Electrical messages are sent along the nerves through the body to and from the brain.

THE NERVOUS SYSTEM

The human nervous system consists of the brain, spinal cord, and a network of nerves. The basic nerve cell is called a **neuron**. This is a specialist cell, with a long extension called an **axon**. Lots of smaller extensions link the neuron to many other neurons, creating a complex network.

The neuron is either "on" when it is sending a message or "off" when it is resting. When it is on, an electrical signal is sent speeding down the axon to the end where there is a special junction linking it to another neuron. At the junction, the arrival of the electrical signal causes a chemical to be released, which moves across to the next cell and switches that neuron on. The size of the electrical signal is always the same, but the number of electrical signals that pass along the axon varies. A strong stimulus will generate a lot of electrical signals, while a weak one only produces a few.

Neurons can vary greatly in their size and shape depending upon their function and where they are found in the body.

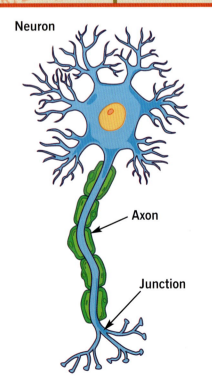

Neuron

Axon

Junction

PROTECTING THE BODY

When you touch a hot object, you pull back your hand without even thinking about it. This is an automatic response, called a **reflex**, that protects the body from injury. First, receptors in your fingertips detect the hot object. Then, electrical messages are instantly sent along sensory neurons to the spinal cord. The message is then carried to muscles in the arm, which contract and pull the hand away from the hot object.

RECENT DEVELOPMENTS
Microchips for prosthetic limbs

A new **microchip** is being developed to allow people with **prosthetic** arms greater control. Many people who have lost their arms still have the ability to send messages to the surrounding muscles. British scientists are building a microchip that can link thought processes in the brain with movements in the prosthetic limb. The microchip is placed in the prosthetic arm. It reads messages arriving at the muscles and instructs the arm to move in a particular way. For example, it can understand messages to open and close the hand and move the elbow and wrist.

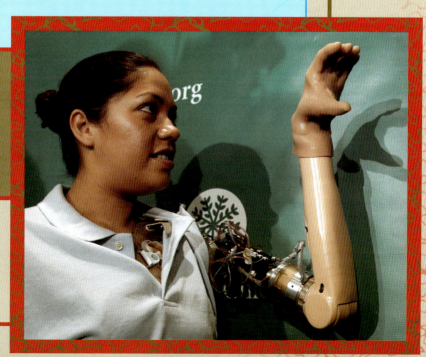

This woman was the first to be fitted with a **bionic** arm. She is able to control parts of her bionic arm and hand using only her thoughts.

ELECTRICITY AND THE BRAIN

There are about 100 billion neurons in the brain, which means there is a lot of electrical activity taking place. The brain can be divided up into different regions, each of which has a different job. Some areas control the heartbeat and blood pressure, and others control balance and coordination. The largest parts of the brain, the cerebral hemispheres, are concerned with thoughts and memories – receiving and processing information from the senses and sending messages to the muscles.

STUDYING BRAIN ACTIVITY

By recording electrical activity, scientists can learn which roles the different parts of the brain play. To record electrical activity, scientists attach sensitive electrodes to different spots on a person's head. The electrodes, which are conductors, pick up electrical activity in the brain and a device records the activity. This is printed on to graph paper that is moving through the machine. The graph is called an **electroencephalograph**, or EEG. By looking at the graph, a doctor can tell whether a person is awake or asleep, whether there is a problem with one part of the brain, and how long it took the brain to respond to a particular stimulus. An EEG can record the tiniest changes in activity. For example, if a person hears a sound, his or her brain's response to that stimulus will be recorded on the graph.

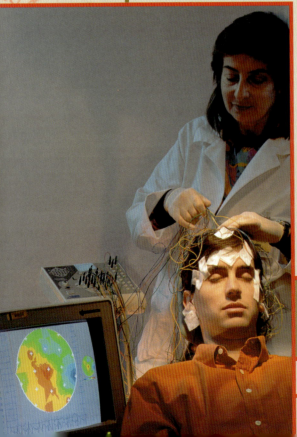

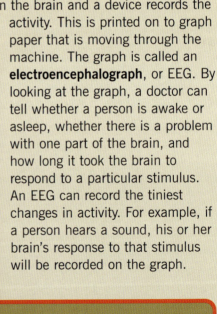

A researcher has fitted electrodes around this patient's head. The electrical activity of the different parts of the brain is shown on the computer screen.

ELECTRIC SHOCK

An electric shock is dangerous because an electric current entering the body from an outside source will **override** the body's nervous system. As the electric current flows through the body it stops messages from the brain, which prevents the use of the body's muscles. For example, a person who touches a faulty appliance may not be able to let go because they cannot control the muscles in their arm. An electric shock can cause serious burns and may even stop a person's heart.

If you see a person who is being shocked by a strong electric current, do not try to pull the person away from the source unless the electricity is turned off. If you touch the person while the electricity is on, the current will pass through the person and into your body. The only safe way to disconnect someone from an electric current is using a non-conducting material such as a wooden stick or plastic pole. This should only be done once the electricity has been switched off!

CASE STUDY Electroconvulsive therapy

Believe it or not, some mental disorders can be treated by passing an electric current through the brain. This treatment is called electroconvulsive therapy, and it is sometimes used to treat severe depression in patients for whom all other forms of treatment have failed.

In electroconvulsive therapy, the patient is anaesthetized and an electrode is placed on either side of the head. Then an electric current of about 800 milliamps (eight-tenths of one amp) is passed through the patient's brain for a few seconds. The patient usually has a series of treatments.

Although electroconvulsive therapy has been in use since the 1930s, doctors are still uncertain of why it works, so it is a very controversial treatment. In addition to this, the effects are short-lived, so people need regular treatments, which can cause memory loss.

ELECTRICITY AND THE HEART

Electrical signals keep your heart pumping blood throughout your body. A certain electrical signal tells the muscles in the heart's upper two chambers (the atria) to tighten, or contract. This pushes blood into the two lower chambers (the ventricles) of the heart. Once the lower chambers are filled with blood, a second electrical signal causes them to contract. As a result, blood is pushed out to the rest of the body.

In a healthy person, this process is repeated between 60 and 100 times a minute. This is your heart rate. When you exercise, your muscles need more of the oxygen that is carried in your blood, so your heart's electrical system speeds up.

CASE STUDY Pacemakers

Some people suffer from too slow a heart rate. They experience dizzy spells, fainting, and fatigue because too little blood is being pumped around their body. This can be treated by using a device called a **pacemaker** to control the heart rate. The pacemaker monitors the beating of the heart and, if it is too slow, it sends a message to speed up the heart rate. It is a tiny device consisting of a generator and a lead. The generator is really a tiny sealed computer chip powered by a battery and sealed in a case the size of a coin. It is inserted into the chest wall and the leads run from the generator along a vein to the heart.

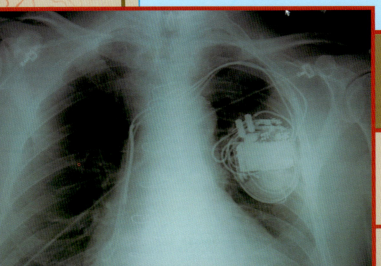

This computerized X-ray shows a pacemaker in a person's body.

CHECKING THE HEART

The electrical activity in the heart can be recorded by an **electrocardiogram**, or ECG. Electrodes from an ECG machine are placed on the patient's chest, and the electrical activity of the heart is recorded on a graph that shows a series of peaks, each of which corresponds to a heartbeat. By looking at the shape of the peaks and the time between them, doctors can determine whether there is a problem with the heart or even if the person has had a heart attack. Sometimes, the patient is asked to walk or run on a treadmill, so that the heart's activity during exercise can be monitored.

EMERGENCY MEDICINE

How many times have you seen a hospital drama where a patient's heart stops and the medics get the heart beating again by giving the patient an electric shock? The electric shock is produced by a device called a **defibrillator**. Although an electric shock can kill or harm a person, the shock from a defibrillator is just sufficient to reset the electric signals in the heart and get it pumping again. A defibrillator consists of two electrodes, called paddles, and an electric unit that generates the shocks. One paddle is placed on the right side of the chest, the other on the lower left side. When the circuit is complete, the electricity flows through the body and restarts the heart.

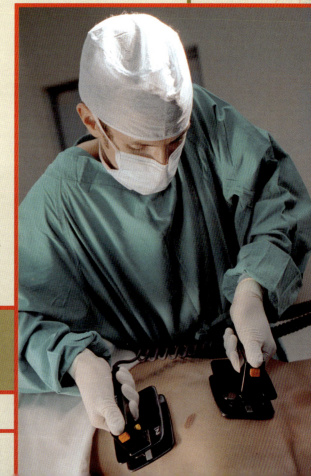

A defibrillator produces just the right amount of shock to restart the heart, without harming the patient.

NAVIGATION AND HUNTING

Most animals produce electricity in their nerves, but some generate electricity for other reasons. Animals such as electric catfish, electric eels, and torpedo rays generate electricity to navigate in murky water, or even to use as a weapon.

ELECTROLOCATION

Some fish use electric signals to navigate in the water. This is called electrolocation. One such fish is the elephant nose fish, which is named after its trunk-like nose. The elephant nose fish lives in murky water where good eyesight is of little use. Instead, the fish emits weak pulses of electricity into the water. These electric pulses, which are not strong enough to stun prey, are used to generate an electric field around the fish. Special receptors over the surface of the fish's body pick up any disturbances in the electric field. From this information they can judge the distances of objects in the water. Many electric fish also use electric signals to communicate with other electric fish and to find mates.

LOOKING FOR POLLUTION

Scientists have discovered that electric fish are very sensitive to tiny amounts of pollutants in the water, so they can be used as pollution monitors. In this case, a fish is placed in water

and its electrical signals are recorded. When the fish encounters polluted water, the number of electrical signals it emits increases considerably so the scientists know the water is polluted.

The elephant nose fish is used to test the quality of drinking water in countries such as Germany and the United States. When the water quality decreases, the number of electrical pulses produced by the fish increases.

This electric catfish hunts at night. It uses its electric weapon to stun its prey, and then it kills and eats the fish.

ELECTRIC WEAPONS

Africa's freshwater electric catfish and the electric eels found in South America use electricity as a weapon. Both animals have an electric organ, which is a layer of specially modified muscle lying under the skin of the body and tail. This electric organ takes up more than four-fifths of the fish's body. The cells that make up the organ are specially adapted to generate electricity, with each cell capable of producing 0.15V. Together, these cells can produce the high voltages needed to kill the fish's prey.

Some of the larger electric fish, which grow to 2.5 metres (8.2 feet) in length, can generate a jolt of electricity that is between 300V and 600V – enough to seriously injure a human. These fish can vary the size of the electrical output, using lower voltages to locate prey and then using the powerful high voltage to stun or kill it.

Did you know..?

Archaeologists have found ancient Egyptian **hieroglyphics** describing the electric catfish, which is found in the River Nile. The Egyptians feared this large fish because of its ability to stun a person wading in the water.

Plugging in

Most of the electricity that we use in our homes is generated by power stations that run on fossil fuels such as coal, oil, and gas. However, it is also possible to generate electricity using nuclear energy and renewable energy sources, such as wind, sunlight, and water, or by simply burning wood.

Although different sources of energy can be used to generate electricity, most power stations use the principle of electromagnetic **induction** to produce the electricity. They do this with a machine called a generator, which converts mechanical energy into electrical energy.

GENERATORS

Inside a generator there is a large magnet and a coil of wire. As the wire spins in the magnetic field of the magnet, the magnetic force pushes electrons along the coil. The electrons flow in one direction as the coil rotates 180 degrees, but for the next 180 degrees the magnetic force reverses and the electrons flow in the opposite direction. This means that as the coil moves the current changes direction twice each rotation, producing an alternating current.

The energy that moves the coil in the generator is usually provided by another machine called a turbine. A turbine consists of blades that are spun by steam, wind, or water. The energy created by the spinning blades of the turbines is used to spin the coil of wire in the generator.

Did you know..?

There are so many electric lights burning at night in major cities that people living there never see a true night sky.

SCIENCE PIONEERS
Michael Faraday: Electromagnetic Induction

British scientist Michael Faraday (1791–1867) carried out many experiments into electricity and magnetism. One of his most important discoveries was finding a way of combining movement and magnetism to generate electricity. By moving a magnet in and out of a coil of wire, he found he could convert the movement energy of the magnet into electrical energy in the wire. This is called electromagnetic induction. Faraday had made the first simple electric generator.

There are various types of turbine. A steam turbine uses the pressure of steam to move the blades, and a gas turbine uses the pressure from expanding gas to turn the blades. A wind turbine uses the force from wind to spin the blades. Hydroelectric dams have water turbines positioned at the bottom of a dam or a long pipe, which are spun by the force of falling water.

Hoover Dam was built across the Colorado River, on the border between Arizona and Utah, USA, creating Lake Mead. There are 17 huge turbines and generators (see below) in the dam that generate 2,000 megawatts of electrical power.

A COAL-FIRED POWER STATION

Coal is still one of the most commonly used fuels for generating electricity. It is a relatively cheap fuel that is mined around the world. Huge quantities of coal are required to generate sufficient electricity to power a city, and it is usually transported by train, ship, or barge. A coal train may bring in 10,000 tonnes at a time, which is enough to last a large power station about a day. In times of high demand as many as three train loads may be required. Demand is higher during extreme cold weather or during a heatwave when more people are using air conditioning.

INSIDE THE FURNACE

At the power station, the coal is crushed into a powder, which is blown into the furnace. When coal burns in air it releases vast quantities of heat, which is used to boil water circulating through pipes around the furnace. The steam is separated and heated further to produce very high-pressure steam, which is then piped to the turbine room.

As it passes through the turbines, the high-pressure steam provides the force to spin the blades. The turbines are connected to huge electromagnets in the generators. The spinning electromagnets cause an electric current to form in the wires that surround the coils. The steam that leaves the turbine is still quite hot, so it is piped to cooling towers where it cools down and condenses back to water. The steam that escapes before it can condense back into water forms the clouds that are often seen coming out of the towers.

DIRTY FUEL

Coal is a relatively dirty fuel. When coal burns it produces gases such as **sulphur dioxide**, which is a major cause of **acid rain**. Luckily, this gas can be removed using special filters in the chimneys. Oil burns more cleanly than coal, and gas is the cleanest of all the fossil fuels. Oil and gas also burn more efficiently than coal, so less is needed to achieve the same level of electrical output. However, fossil fuels are not renewable and they are being used up. Soon supplies will run out so we need alternative ways to generate electricity.

SOLAR ENERGY

A good alternative to coal is solar energy, or energy from the Sun. One way of using solar energy to generate electricity is through the use of photovoltaic cells. Photovoltaic cells contain a material such as silicon – a light-sensitive material that generates a small electric current when placed in sunlight. A photovoltaic panel consists of many cells, each generating a small current of electricity.

Modern photovoltaic cells are only able to convert about 17 percent of the gathered sunlight into electricity. However, advances in technology mean this number is improving all the time. Using solar energy to generate electricity is expensive, but many people feel it is worth the cost. Solar energy does not require the burning of fossil fuels (which is linked to pollution and global climate change) and it is a renewable source of energy. It is ideal for remote places that are far away from a power station, and for applications that do not require a lot of power such as telephones.

These photovoltaic cells are being used to provide power to a remote village in the Himalayas.

TRANSMITTING ELECTRICITY

A power station is just one part of the infrastructure that is required to get electricity to end users. Once electricity is generated, it has to be transmitted across the country via a network of cables and transmission towers, called pylons.

PYLONS

Sometimes electricity from power stations has to be transmitted over long distances. For example, wind farms (which use wind turbines to generate electricity) are often built in remote places, but most electricity is needed in cities and industrial areas. In this case, overhead cables supported by a network of pylons may be used to carry the electricity. Sometimes underground cables are used instead but, since this is more expensive than an overhead system, this does not happen very often.

When electricity flows along a cable it encounters resistance, which causes energy to be lost as heat (see page 20). The amount of resistance that is met increases with the length of the cable, as does the amount of energy that is lost as heat. Electricity companies that deliver electricity over very long distances need to make the loss of energy as small as possible.

TRANSFORMERS

In any conductor the energy loss is smaller if the voltage is larger, so it makes sense to use as high a voltage as practical – ideally hundreds of thousands of volts. Of course, ordinary homes cannot cope with that high a voltage, so a device called a **transformer** is needed. A transformer can increase the voltage for efficient transport and get it back down to a manageable level for use in homes.

Power station generators produce electricity at about 25,000V, and then step-up transformers convert it to 275,000V and 400,000V for transmission. Once the electricity reaches the city or industrial zone, it is converted back to a lower voltage using a step-down transformer. For example, houses in the United Kingdom get their electricity at 240V; in the United States it is 110V.

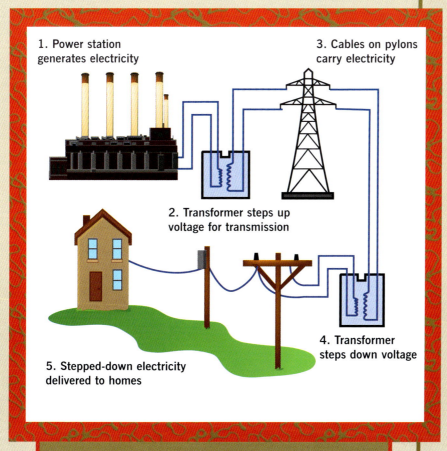

1. Power station generates electricity

3. Cables on pylons carry electricity

2. Transformer steps up voltage for transmission

4. Transformer steps down voltage

5. Stepped-down electricity delivered to homes

Electricity is generated at the power station. A step-up transformer converts the 25,000V current to 275,000V for transmission over long-distance wires. At the step-down transformer, the current is reduced to a voltage that is safe for home use.

RECENT DEVELOPMENTS Supergrid

There are plans to develop a supergrid that would carry electricity at voltages in excess of 400,000V so that there is virtually no loss of energy. The supergrid would be built using superconductors. However, most superconductors only work at very low temperatures, so the cables would have to be buried and cooled – probably by liquid hydrogen.

HAZARDOUS BY-PRODUCTS

The generation of electricity has always caused considerable pollution of land, water, and air – and it continues to do so today. The worst culprits are power stations that burn fossil fuels, especially those that burn coal.

ACID RAIN

Coal contains many impurities, such as sulphur. When the coal is burnt, the waste gas sulphur dioxide is produced. Sulphur dioxide is one of the main causes of acid rain. Although many power stations have installed filters to prevent sulphur dioxide from being released into the atmosphere, considerable damage has already been done to forests and lakes, especially in Europe, and damage is still occurring in less developed parts of the world.

GLOBAL WARMING

Carbon dioxide is another by-product of power stations that burn fossil fuels and biomass such as wood and straw. Carbon dioxide is a greenhouse gas. It is one of several gases that trap the Sun's heat within Earth's atmosphere. When the right

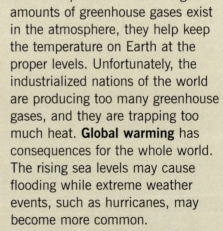

amounts of greenhouse gases exist in the atmosphere, they help keep the temperature on Earth at the proper levels. Unfortunately, the industrialized nations of the world are producing too many greenhouse gases, and they are trapping too much heat. **Global warming** has consequences for the whole world. The rising sea levels may cause flooding while extreme weather events, such as hurricanes, may become more common.

This tree was killed by acid rain that was created by the nearby power station.

RADIOACTIVE WASTE

Nuclear power is another source of energy that is used to generate electricity. Currently, about 19 percent of the world's electricity is produced in this way. In some countries, such as France and Sweden, nuclear power is the main energy source. Nuclear power stations produce very little carbon dioxide and they don't produce any sulphur dioxide – but they do produce **radioactive** waste. Radioactive waste is incredibly harmful to all living things and requires very careful disposal.

CLEAN ELECTRICITY

The only really clean form of electricity comes from renewable energy sources such as wind, water, **geothermal** (heat from inside the Earth), and solar energy. Though increasing amounts of electricity are being generated from these sources, they still only account for a small percentage of electricity produced worldwide.

These turbines are harnessing the power of the wind to create electricity cleanly.

CASE STUDY Powering developing nations

As the standard of living improves in many less-developed countries of the world, the demand for electricity increases. Many countries are turning to renewable sources to supply power. Small-scale projects, such as installing small solar power stations and mini-hydro schemes on mountain rivers, are sufficient to supply power to villages.

Using electrical energy

Imagine trying to build a house with hand tools. Even a simple task such as making a hole in the wall would take time and effort. Today, an electric drill makes the job so much easier and quicker. This is possible because electrical energy can be changed into mechanical energy. Electrical energy can also be changed into other forms of energy, such as sound and light.

ENERGY CHANGES

There is an important law in physics, which states that no energy change is 100 percent efficient. That means that when you are changing one form of energy into another, some of the energy will be lost as heat.

A good example of this is when electricity is changed into light. The most common type of light bulb is an incandescent bulb – it gives off heat as well as light. This glass bulb contains a long, thin length of tungsten wire. When electricity passes along the wire the tungsten becomes so hot that it glows, giving off light. However, it also gives off a lot of heat. In fact, nearly all the electrical energy is changed to heat – less than 10 percent is actually changed into light – so it is a very inefficient way to produce light.

An incandescent bulb, such as this one, uses energy inefficiently – much of it is lost as heat.

One of the most efficient energy changes is changing electrical energy to heat energy as in an electric fire. About 97 percent of the energy is converted to heat and the rest is changed to other forms of energy, such as light. Car engines are far less efficient, with only 25 to 30 percent of the chemical energy of the fuel being changed to the movement that turns the wheels.

CASE STUDY Converting electricity to sound

Electricity is essential for microphones and loudspeakers. In a microphone, the sound energy is converted to electrical signals. As a person speaks into the microphone, the sound waves cause a membrane to vibrate and this creates an electric current of varying strength in the wire. The electric signals are strengthened and carried along the wire to a loudspeaker where there is an electromagnet. The differing strength of the current makes the magnetic field stronger or weaker, which pulls on a metal disc more or less. The vibrations in the disc create sound waves that are replicas of the original sound waves. In a loudspeaker, the sound waves are made louder by attaching a cardboard cone to the metal disc. The cone vibrates too and creates a louder sound.

Sounds produced by the singer and her guitar are picked up by the microphones and converted into electrical signals, which are transmitted to the huge loudspeakers at the back of the stage. The speakers convert the electrical signals to sound.

SAVING ELECTRICITY

Every year, new power stations are built to meet the growing worldwide demand for electricity. This could be avoided if people reduced their electricity consumption. One way to achieve this is by improving the efficiency of energy changes. That might mean that an appliance would require less electricity to do its job, or it could mean that a power station generates more electricity for each tonne of fuel.

Fluorescent tubes, which are more efficient than incandescent bulbs, are another way to save energy. Fluorescent tubes are filled with a gas such as argon, neon, or mercury vapour. When the light is switched on, electrons pass through the gas, bumping into the gas **molecules** and causing them to give off ultraviolet light. This causes a chemical on the inside of the tube to glow, which produces a white light.

Low-energy light bulbs or compact fluorescent lamps are even more efficient. These lights use only about one-fifth the electricity used by a tungsten bulb. That is because they generate less heat while producing the same amount of light. Although they are more expensive than traditional bulbs, these low-energy bulbs last longer. A low-energy bulb typically lasts between 8,000 and 15,000 hours. An incandescent bulb lasts only about 1,000 hours.

Did you know..?

If you replaced one incandescent 100W light bulb in your home with an equivalent low-energy bulb, in a year you would save enough electricity to boil 200 litres (52 gallons) of water and make 1,200 cups of coffee. Imagine how much electricity could be saved if everybody swapped their traditional light bulbs for low-energy ones!

ENERGY RATINGS

Electrical goods such as refrigerators, freezers, and washing machines are rated according to the amount of electricity they use. For example, in Europe, appliances are rated from A to G, with A being the most efficient. This gives the purchaser information to help them choose the most energy-efficient model. Fridges and freezers can be made more efficient by having increased insulation and good door seals, while washing machines can use less water and use domestic hot water, rather than having their own heaters.

EFFICIENT HEATING

Many homes have a boiler that supplies hot water for washing and heating. A boiler produces a lot of waste heat that goes straight outside. A better option is a micro-combined heat and power (CHP) system. A micro-CHP plant is like a mini power station in the home. Fuel is burnt to power a generator that produces electricity while providing heating and hot water at the same time. Such systems are about 90 percent efficient, which means 90 percent of the energy in the fuel is changed to useful forms of energy. If all homes and businesses had such a system, as much as 25 percent of a country's electricity could be generated in this way.

CASE STUDY Standby power

Many appliances and electrical devices continue to use power even when they are turned off. Items such as a microwave oven or DVD player use standby power to keep their clocks running while the power is off. Other items, such as a TV or computer, use standby power so that they can be switched on in an instant. Recent studies have shown that standby power accounts for between 10 and 13 percent of a household's total power consumption. One report estimates that the standby power used annually by the United States equals all of the electricity used by Peru, Vietnam, and Greece combined!

CLEANER CARS

Traditional vehicles are not good for the environment because they pollute the air and require fossil fuels to run. Concerns about global climate change and the rising costs of oil have led to the development of electric and **hybrid** cars.

ELECTRIC CARS

From the outside, an electric car looks the same as a petrol or diesel car. It sounds very different, though, because it runs quietly. Instead of an engine under the bonnet, there is a large battery pack, an electric motor, and a controller for the motor. The job of the controller is to take the power from the battery and deliver it to the motor. The driver controls the amount of power that is delivered to the motor in the same way as with a traditional vehicle. When the driver pushes down on the accelerator pedal, the controller supplies more power to the motor. When the driver lifts their foot from the pedal, the power is cut.

Instead of refuelling the engine with petrol or diesel, the driver of an electric car has to recharge the battery, which can take several hours. Currently, batteries are the main restriction on the use of electric cars because they have a limited range and are heavy, expensive, and quickly worn out. Electric cars are ideal for use in towns and cities, but are not as good for long-distance journeys.

The motors used in electric and hybrid cars look quite similar to the motors used in petrol-powered cars.

RECENT DEVELOPMENTS Tesla Roadster

One of the disadvantages of the early electric cars was that they did not go very fast. But a new sports car is changing that. The Tesla Roadster is a small sports car that is 100 percent electric. Thanks to a state-of-the-art lithium ion battery, the car can run for more than 400 kilometres (250 miles) before its battery needs recharging. The Tesla Roadster is also a high-performance car, able to accelerate from 0 to 96 kilometres (60 miles) per hour in less than 4 seconds – that's faster than a Porsche 911!

The Tesla Roadster is attracting a lot of attention. Not only is it a stylish and fast car – it is all electric. The battery can be completely charged in just a few hours.

HYBRID CARS

A good alternative to an electric car is a hybrid, which combines a conventional engine with a battery and motor. Hybrids do not have the same limitations as electric cars and are also manufactured in greater numbers than electric cars. These types of vehicle are becoming increasingly popular, especially in cities such as Los Angeles, USA, where there are strict emission controls for cars. When the vehicle is travelling at low speeds, the battery powers the motor. As the vehicle's speed increases to more than 48 kilometres (30 miles) per hour, the engine takes over and powers the car while it recharges the battery. The hybrid car is cheaper to run than a conventional car, getting up to three times more kilometres to the litre, and it produces less pollution.

ELECTROCHEMISTRY

Have you ever wondered what the terms "silver-plated" or "gold-plated" mean? They refer to a thin layer of silver or gold being laid over another metal. The manufacturing process is called **electroplating** and it is just one example of how electricity can bring about useful chemical reactions.

When an electric current is passed through an **electrolyte**, a liquid that conducts electricity, the electricity triggers a chemical reaction. For example, passing an electric current through slightly acidic water causes the water to break up into oxygen and hydrogen gases. Passing an electric current through a strong salt solution breaks the solution down into hydrogen and chlorine gases. The process of using electricity to create a chemical reaction is called **electrolysis**, and it has many industrial uses including extracting metals from rock and coating metals with layers of silver and chrome.

ELECTROPLATING

Electroplating is done to either make a metal look more attractive, as is the case with silver-plated objects, or to protect it from rusting. For example, steel rusts when it gets wet so it is protected by a layer of zinc. This type of steel is called galvanized steel. Chrome is also used to protect steel. In fact, bicycle frames are often made from steel coated with chrome for a shiny finish that will not rust. The only way the metal will rust is if the protective coating is damaged and water is allowed to reach the steel below.

A silver-plated object is usually made from an inexpensive metal such as nickel, which is then covered in a layer of silver. To accomplish this, the nickel object and a rod of silver metal are suspended in an electrolyte during the manufacturing process. Then an electric current is passed through the silver into the electrolyte and out through the nickel. The current causes a layer of silver to form on the nickel. When the layer has reached the desired thickness, the current is switched off and the object is removed.

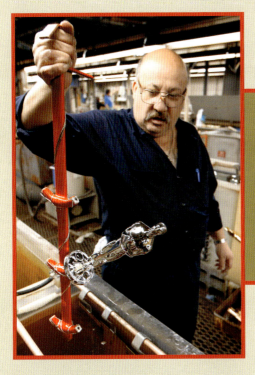

This man is using the process of electroplating on an Oscar statue. The Oscars are one of the top awards in the film industry. Each statue is plated with copper, silver, nickel, and 24-carat gold to give it an extra shine.

EXTRACTING METALS

Many metals do not naturally exist on their own. Instead they are found inside rocks called ores. For example, aluminium is obtained from the ore bauxite. The metal has to be extracted from the ore, a process that can be achieved by electrolysis. A lot of electricity is needed for this process, though, which contributes significantly to the cost of producing aluminium. It is much cheaper and more environmentally friendly to recycle aluminium from cans and other items than to quarry bauxite.

Did you know..?

The cans that are used for food are made from steel covered with a thin layer of tin. Tin is a safe metal to place in contact with food. It also stops the contents of the can from rusting the steel, and keeps the can bright and shiny.

Electricity and the future

Scientists continue to research ways of generating and using electricity. Electrical circuits are being improved, and the **microprocessors** used in computers and other hi-tech equipment are getting smaller and more powerful. Microprocessors are also being used in robots, which are becoming increasingly complex.

BIG BROTHER IS WATCHING

For many years, pets and some livestock have been "chipped". That is, a computer chip about the size of a grain of rice is injected under the skin. The chip carries information on the identity of the animal, which can be programmed and read using short-range radio signals. The technology is called RF Identity, or RFID. The latest RFID chips can store far more information, and even do calculations. In the future, even people may have RFID chips implanted. The chip could contain information on the person's health, bank details, credit ratings, and much more. The chips could also be used for other purposes. For example, criminals could have an RFID chip inserted into their skin and special sensors would be used to track their location.

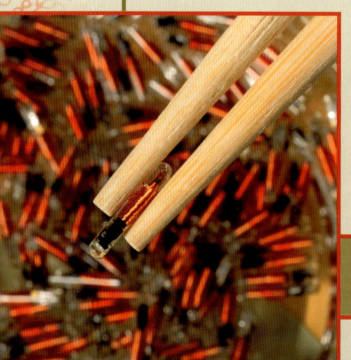

An RFID chip is held by a pair of chopsticks. The chip can be used to store security, financial, and emergency information.

FASTER SPACE TRAVEL

Research is taking place to design new engines that can take spacecraft to Mars and beyond. Currently, the journey time to Mars and back is just over two years. It is hoped that the new engines will reduce this time to just three months. In 2006, the European Space Agency developed a **prototype** engine, called an ion engine, which is claimed to be up to 10 times more efficient than existing engines. The ion engine produces an electric field that pushes a beam of positively charged particles away from the spacecraft, propelling the spacecraft forwards.

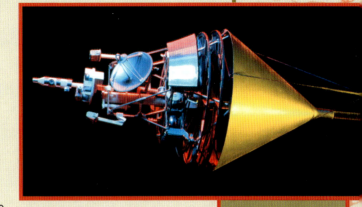

This is a model of a space probe that is fitted with an ion engine. In the future this probe might be used to study the Sun.

NANO-ELECTRONICS

Thanks to advances in micro-processing skills, the components used on computer chips are getting very small – so small that engineers are now working at the level of the atom. This field of engineering is called nanotechnology and it involves engineering things that are smaller than 100 nanometres. To give you an idea of how small that is – one nanometre is one-billionth of a metre!

Scientists discovered that the presence of impurities in a semiconductor can make it conduct electricity more quickly, so they purposely added impurities in the manufacturing process. For example, arsenic may be added to silicon. This can be tricky, though, because the atoms of arsenic are randomly scattered through the semiconductor. When the size of the semiconductor is so tiny, this lack of uniformity can cause problems. To rectify this problem, scientists are now experimenting with using a beam to insert individual atoms into a semiconductor at regular intervals of about 60 nanometres, in order to improve the performance of the semiconductor.

ROBOTS

For many years, robots were a staple of science-fiction films. However, for the past 40 years or so, robots have been appearing in the workplace. Robots are usually computer-controlled machines that are used to carry out routine jobs. For example, robotic arms are used in car factories to weld and to paint the cars. The job is repeated over and over again with great precision. Robots can also be used in places that are dangerous for humans, such as in bomb disposal. Robots also play an important role in space exploration. In January 2004, two National Aeronautics and Space Administration (NASA) rovers landed on Mars. They were supposed to last for three months, but were still going strong three years later.

ANDROIDS

With the latest advancements in microtechnology, which involves the miniaturization of circuits, it has become possible to build robots that can carry out a greater range of tasks. Some of the latest generation of robots have been given a human-like appearance. These are called androids.

A typical android has a metal skeleton with joints so that the different limbs can move. It also has a motor, a sensor system, a power supply, and a control centre. The limbs are moved using **actuators**. Most actuators are mini-motors, especially those in the hand. All the actuators are wired into an electric circuit that connects them to the power source, which is either a battery or the mains. The control centre is also part of the circuit. Programs controlling the behaviour of the robot are downloaded into the control centre.

Did you know..?

Italian artist and inventor Leonardo da Vinci (1452–1519) made one of the first drawings of a human-like robot in about 1495. His notebook contained detailed drawings of a mechanical knight in armour that was able to sit up and wave its arms.

Androids that can move around need to have information about their surroundings so they do not bump into obstacles. This information is usually gathered by sensors that feed data back to the android.

SCIENCE PIONEERS
Hiroshi Ishiguro: Geminoid

In 2006 Japanese Professor Hiroshi Ishiguro built an android that looked just like him. Professor Ishiguro builds robots that look like people because he feels that they will work better in the human environment and that they will be more acceptable to people. Professor Ishiguro believes that robots will help us understand more about ourselves. The mechanical "skeleton" of his robots are covered in a soft silicone layer coloured to look like skin and then given a wig, make-up, and clothes.

Professor Hiroshi Ishiguro with his android called "Geminoid". This android will be used in research to find out how an android can be given the personality of a real person.

ELECTRICITY — PAST, PRESENT, AND FUTURE

Electricity has come a long way from the time when scientists discovered how to produce a continuous flow of electricity. Today, it is an essential source of energy in every home and office. Despite the environmental problems linked to our use of electricity, it is likely to remain central to our lives, even as the way in which it is generated changes.

Further resources

MORE BOOKS TO READ

Horrible Science: Killer Energy and Shocking Electricity,
Nick Arnold and Tony de Saulles (Scholastic Hippo, 2006)

Making Sense of Science: Electricity and Power, Peter Riley
(Franklin Watts, 2005)

Science Files: Electricity and Magnetism, Steve Parker
(Heinemann Library, 2005)

Science Investigations: Electricity, John Farndon (Hodder
Wayland, 2006)

*Science Stories: Adventures with Electricity: Benjamin
Franklin's Story*, Beverley Birch (Matthew Price, 2006)

USING THE INTERNET

Explore the Internet to find out more about electricity. You can
use a search engine such as kids.yahoo.com and type in
keywords such as static electricity, current electricity,
electromagnetism, renewable energy, or electrocardiogram.

These search tips will help you find useful websites more
quickly:

• Know exactly what you want to find out about first.

• Use only a few important keywords in a search, putting
  the most relevant words first.

• Be precise. Only use names of people, places, or things.

Glossary

acid rain   rain that contains acidic pollutants

actuator   mechanism that moves an object

alternating current   current that changes directions many times every second

ammeter   device for measuring an electrical current

ampere   unit of measurement of an electric current, also called an amp

atom   unit of matter out of which everything is made

axon   long extension of a nerve cell that carries messages to the next nerve cell

battery   store of electrical charges

bionic   having part of the body replaced by an artificial structure with electronic components

circuit   path of an electrical current along wires

circuit breaker   switch that stops the flow of electricity in case of an electrical overload or some other problem

compressor   machine that is used to compress (squash) air or other gases

conduction   flow of electricity through a conductor such as metal

conductor   material that allows heat or electrical energy to pass through it

current   flow of electrons, measured in amperes

current electricity   electricity that flows along a wire and through a circuit

defibrillator   electronic device used to establish a normal heartbeat

direct current   current that flows in one direction all the time

electrical discharge   sudden loss of excess charge from an object

electrocardiogram   test that records electrical activity of the heart

electrode   conductor through which electricity enters or leaves a system

electroencephalograph   machine that records brainwave activity

electrolysis   chemical reaction caused by the passing of an electric current through an electrolyte

electrolyte   liquid that conducts electricity

electromagnet   magnet created by electricity

electron   negatively charged particle in an atom

electroplating   using electricity to cover an object with a thin layer of metal

energy   ability to do work

force   push or pull that gives energy to an object

fossil fuel   carbon-rich fuel, such as oil, gas, or coal, made millions of years ago from the remains of living organisms

friction   resistance that occurs when two objects or substances are moved over each other

fuse   safety device – a length of wire in a circuit that melts when the current is too large, breaking the circuit

generator   machine that creates electricity

geothermal   energy from inside Earth

global warming   gradual warming of Earth's climate through an increase in greenhouse gases such as carbon dioxide and methane

grounding   connecting an electrical circuit to the Earth via a length of wire at the circuit breaker box. This makes sure that any electrical charges flow safely away to the Earth if the circuit breaker is tripped by a fault on the circuit.

hieroglyphics   picture writing used by the ancient Egyptians

hybrid   mix or cross

induction   producing a voltage in a wire by changing the magnetic field around it, such as by moving a magnet past it

insulator   material that does not allow electricity to pass through it

magnetic field   field of force around a magnet or an electromagnet

magnetic levitation   lifting an object off the ground using magnetic repulsion

magnetism   force of attraction between a magnet and another object

mass   measure of the amount of matter in a substance

matter   substance or material

microchip   small piece of silicon carrying microscopic circuits

microprocessor   central processing unit consisting of a silicon chip with integrated circuits found in computers, digital cameras, and many other electronic devices

molecule   substance composed of two or more atoms held together by chemical bonds

motor   machine that converts electrical energy into mechanical energy

nerve   bundle of fibres that conducts electrical signals around the body

neuron   specialized cell that carries electrical signals

neutron   particle in an atom that has no charge

nuclear power   using the energy released when atoms are either split (nuclear fission) or joined (nuclear fusion) to generate electricity

nucleus   heavy centre of an atom, made up of neutrons and protons

orbit   path that one object makes around another object in space

override   take over

pacemaker   small battery placed under the skin with wires that lead to the heart. It measures heart rate and corrects a heartbeat that is too fast or too slow.

photovoltaic cell   device that converts light energy to electricity. It contains a light–sensitive material such as silicon.

prosthetic   artificial limb

proton   positively charged particle found in an atom

prototype   first model of something that requires further development

radioactive   giving out high-energy waves, rays, or particles

reflex   automatic response such as blinking, coughing, or pulling the hand away from a hot object

renewable   able to be replaced or renewed. This includes resources such as trees, wind energy, and solar energy.

repel   push away

resistance   slowing down of a flow of electrons along a conductor

resistor   electrical component that limits or regulates the flow of electricity in a circuit

semiconductor   material that is neither a good conductor nor a good insulator. Silicon is an example of a semiconductor.

solenoid   coil of wire that becomes a magnet when an electric current is passed through it

static electricity   electric charge that builds up due to friction

sulphur dioxide   chemical by-product created by the burning of fossil fuels, especially coal

superconductor   material that allows a current of electricity to flow with no resistance at very low temperatures

synthetic   artificial

transformer   device used to increase or decrease the voltage of an electric current

turbine   device that consists of a bladed wheel that is turned by the force of moving water, gas, or steam

voltage   unit of the force with which electrons are pushed along a wire

watt   unit of electrical power

Index